THE FREE AGENT

THE PLAYBOOK FOR THE TECHNICAL PROFESSIONAL

BY KARLA TANKERSLEY

Library of Congress Cataloging-in-Publication Data

Tankersley, Karla S.

The Free Agent Playbook for the Technical Professional/ Karla Tankersley

ISBN-13:978-1478277255

IBSN-10:1478277254

1. Non-Fiction 2. Business & Investing 3. Careers 4. Business Industries and Professions 5. High Tech

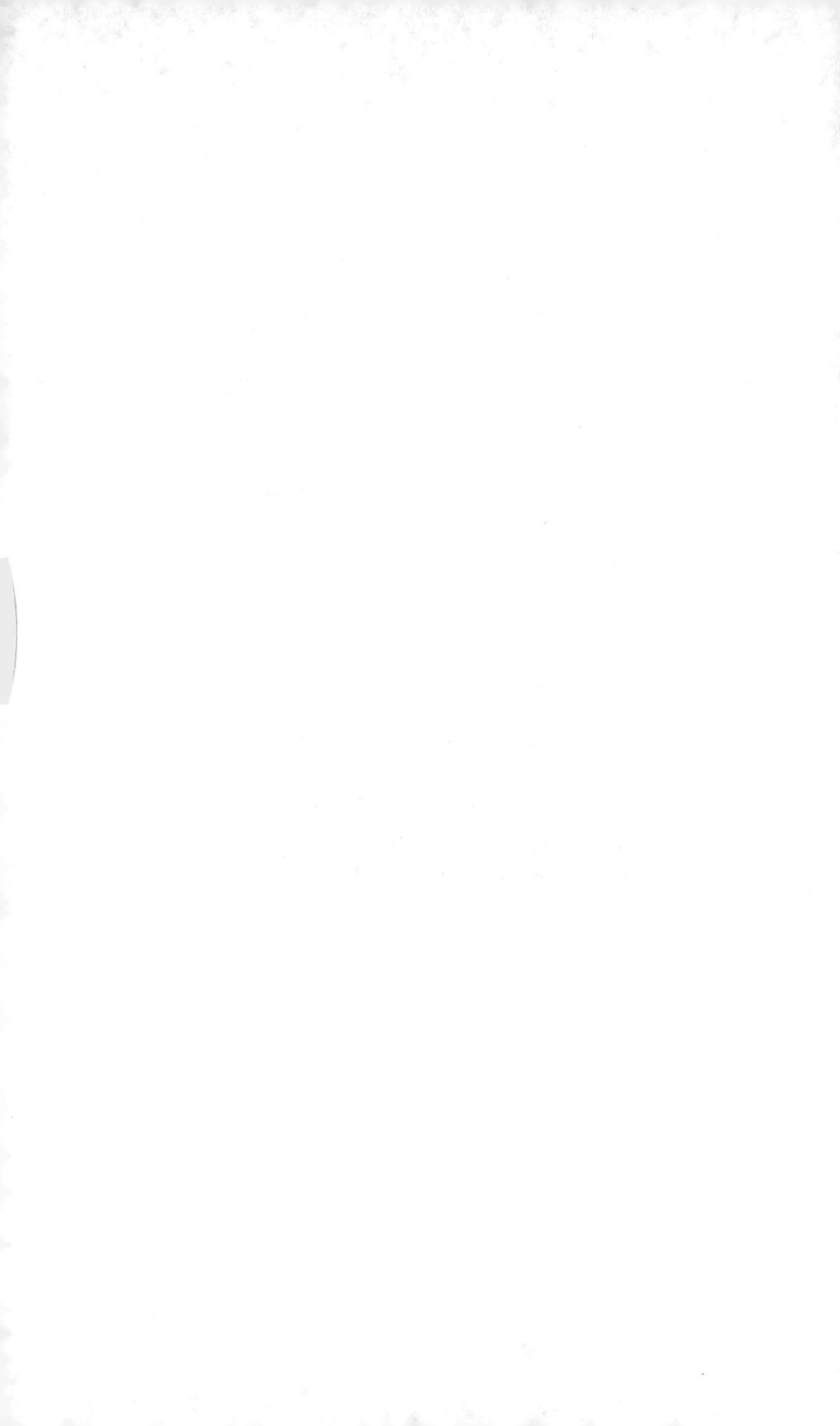

The Free Agent

The Playbook for the Technical Professional

By Karla Tankersley

For Technical Professionals at all levels
of their game

Contents

FOREWORD

Throughout my travels and business ventures, I often get the initial question, what do you do? My response is simple.

I am IE, I get things done.

This usually surprises folks, I think they are expecting some type of a fancy title associated with the household name that I'm currently working for. The title isn't me. The title belongs to the corporation and is really only relevant to those who work there. Only they can understand what department I'm referring to, where I fit in amongst the thousands of employees. Who I am is simple to understand.

I am IE, I get things done.

I was fortunate to have the foresight at a young age to pursue my education in Industrial Engineering. This educational pedigree is who I am, how I think, and what makes me tick. Essentially, these are the tools for how I approach any situation laid before me. I also have a knack for getting things done. Whatever the situation, I can typically get myself and others to move. This is more of the art behind the science of what I do and what makes me tick.

Now, I am no professor and this is certainly no text book. I am no career counselor and do not guarantee any sure success from reading this book. I am no professional or college athlete. I just enjoy the spirit of athletics. You must have some raw talent to be good at it. You must practice and focus to excel at it. There is the team spirit, leadership and outcome that rally the crowd to jump out of their seats and high-five each other.

Why should our careers be different? Mine hasn't. I think that to be worth your weight in the technical arena, you have to bring some raw talent. To be excellent, you must put in the effort, and glean results over time. You make connections, partnerships; create loyal colleagues that span your career. You know when you're on a winning team. You know when you're surrounded by losers who have mentally given up. If your with a winning team, you high-five each other after a job well done and push on to the next game.

This is IE, this is what we do.

It is our time, our opportunity and our greatest mission to be paid to pay, to play at the highest level, and reach our career wins in the sport we love.

Are you ready? The big-time is calling you.

Acknowledgement

This book is a whirl-wind love affair I've been having for the past two years. Sweeping and quickly pulling together page after page from nowhere to create the material you possess today. It's the pure passion for the career that is a sport for me. I play it every day and enjoy every minute of it. I am truly thankful for having the pleasure to work with and for some of the most talented technical professionals of our time. Each of you has influenced me throughout my career and in doing so, I take a piece of you with me. I am thankful for my education. Without the degree in my technical field of Industrial Engineering, I would not be where I am today or even given access to the door into the high-tech companies I've worked for. Throughout the past two years, this creative work has been supported by close colleagues that share my passion for the technical professions. A special thanks to Bob Smyth, Marge Lautar, Clint Crawford, Shawn Curran and Michael Guiliano for your inspiration, motivation and a helpful push when I needed it. I would like to thank my editor, Rob Morner, for his patience, feedback, guidance and directions for somehow making this engineer into a writer. I especially appreciate the love and support of my husband, Stephen Tankersley -- who opened countless doors for me by supporting my desire to go to college. Now our marriage is my rock that gives me the support to be anything I need to be. My son, Elliott James, who is a artist of all mediums and who designs all my cover art. My eldest daughter, Koralyssa, who is captured in the cover of this book, is pursuing her dreams as an Engineer. My daughter, Sarah, who is my great escape with laughter and many hugs. And my baby, Lauren, the caboose of the family, who also is showing the early signs of engineering in her blood. This family is my circle that provides me with love, support, creativity and the relaxation that I sometimes have a hard time finding on my own. Of course, I must thank my sister, Kallie Strobel. No idea is too big with Kallie by my side. She is my best friend and greatest ally in life.

INTRODUCTION

With the first buzz of the
Blackberry at 7 a.m. it's game
time. It's time to get connected
and engaged in this sport that
we call engineering. Yes, I
called engineering a sport.

Engineering is as demanding as
any sport. You must suit up, get
hydrated, practice and pray.

What would America be today
without our beloved sports? Fall

wouldn't be the same without

the air of excitement that comes

from college football. How dull

and grey our winters would be

without basketball. Our fan

pandemonium is contagious, fun

and nostalgic. We paint our

faces and tailgate for our

favorite teams. We dish about

the collective bargaining, fantasy

football and workplace

Brackettville to embellish the fun.

We relish our childhood

memories of little league or that

high school game when we all were coming of age. Of course, throughout the year we also hear about the business side of sports. There are many aspects to the business of sports. From the draft picks of the high school and collegiate talent to the emerging **FREE AGENT**, we can learn how to act in the business world by watching the athletes engaged in the business of sports. Men and women alike update their status on Facebook, post a tweet on Twitter and speed dial their friends from their cell phones when they see their favorite player on the plasma screens during the NFL draft or the latest breaking news about their favorite **FREE AGENT**. As we watch, we see the best of the best -- the young, talented players from all walks of life across the country get selected and **PAID TO PLAY** for a professional team. We see the young man jump from his seat

with his family close at hand as

they walk to a podium to pose

with his pro jersey, team number

and hat. He has just won the

opportunity of a lifetime, the

lottery jackpot for all athletes: he

will get **PAID TO PLAY**. After

years of giving their bodies up

for their sport, they earn the

privilege to become the future

FREE AGENT. Perhaps the

most famous of all Free Agents

in our time is LaBron James.

LaBron has a great American story that warms the heart. LeBron beat the odds to become the youngest player of the NBA with a long list of accolades – Rookie of the Year being only one of them[i]. In high school, with the talent and stature he possessed, he was a true man amongst boys. LeBron successfully made the jump from high school to the National Basketball League. LaBron signed with the Cleveland

Cavaliers as the number one

pick of the NBA draft[iii]. For six

years, LeBron made his mark for

the Cleveland Cavaliers by

playing in 548 games and

producing results. LaBron was

a sound investment. In his

Rookie years with Cleveland, he

averaged 30 points per game.

This firmly set LaBron on the

path of being the most sought-

after **FREE AGENT** of our time.

He became eligible and open for

recruitment in June, 2010. The

professional basketball clubs were anxiously awaiting the moment. When LeBron became eligible, we all watched and thought the same thing: "Let the games begin". Many of us watched ESPN for the daily updates of the clubs poised to bring LaBron and his promise of a national championship to their doorstep. Why all the positioning, politics and posturing to land one player? Because every club knew what

LeBron could bring to their

organization:

TALENT

RESULTS

POTENTIAL

LeBron had the talent to be one

of the best basketball players of

all time. Talent in stature,

athletic ability and prowess in

the sport. He demonstrated

results in the currency that clubs

desire, tangible, measurable

statistics that topped the charts

of ESPN. He had the potential to do more. As a young man at the ripe age of 26, there is mileage left in those sneakers. It's no surprise to many of us who have watched his career that LeBron landed the offer to make $ 14.5 million a year with his new team, the Miami Heat[v].

Of course, there are several Free Agents that get picked up by teams throughout the year. Free Agency became the way of moving players throughout teams in basketball, football and other sports. This concept of being a "Free Agent" was established in baseball in the 1970's. Instead of spending their entire career with one team, an athlete's talent is open to the market to move about with other teams.

Sound familiar? **IT SHOULD**. This parallels closely to our working world. Yes, the average Joes and Janes like us who are not on ESPN. What was once a working world of pensions is now the world of the 401K. The 401K opened the opportunity for the white collar worker to move from company to company and take their retirement plans with them. We are considered the portable white collar workforce . Many of us are just now making the transition of thinking from working for one company your entire adult life to working for the best company, at the right time, and for the right compensation and benefits.

You are a **FREE AGENT**.

You can work for the best company that shares your passion and interests. You can choose to work for the company that has needs and desires that meet the capabilities you possess. You can choose the company that fits your lifestyle and work life integration needs. You can see what the market will bear and choose to work for the company that shares your passion, has the right fit for the time of your career and also will pay you equitably for what you bring to the team.

What we need to understand is the simple economics of the situation. The employment situation of our country as of December 2011 was grim: the unemployment rate was at 8.5 percent[ix]. Of the estimated 153,887,000 American workers, only an estimated 1,571,900 are reported as Engineers[xi]. As you may realize, Engineers make up just slightly over 1% of the working population. We are a rare breed of talent. Imagine if you can the population of professional caliber athletes -- would they comprise 1% of the male population between the ages of 18 and 30? Now, let the games begin ... let's talk **DEMAND**. The profession of engineering is projected to climb by 11%[xii], better than the return on your 401K. Consider that the top corporations of our world are high tech. Topping Fortune's list of Best Companies to Work For are Google, Mercedes-Benz, Intel and others known for their innovation and engineering prowess. Of Fortune's 500, tech is king -- the largest and most successful corporations, such as Amazon, Wal-Mart, Home Depot and Kroger, employ armies of engineers. There has never been a better time to be an engineer. It is our time. Of course, the engineers that are true FREE AGENTS will not box themselves into only engineering. Engineers are the ultimate players in the technical world.

You possess TALENT

You demonstrate RESULTS

You excite others with your POTENTIAL

Companies are taking notice.

Corporations are quickly

learning to identify a **FREE**

AGENT, but also know how to

engage and leverage them to

their advantage. Those

companies who don't know how

to attract and use **FREE**

AGENTS are missing the

strategic advantage that the

technical talent can offer.

We live in a country with a

shrinking workforce. In any

economy, **FREE AGENTS** will

have opportunities. They know it. They don't look for a job; the next opportunity finds them. When you are speaking with several Free Agents, they quickly share their networks. They realize the power of relationships and gaining allies. They receive the phone calls from their extensive network, allies and recruiters. In the social networking world we now live in, they receive taps on the shoulder by those who are fans.

They are shown, like a baseball card, at LinkedIn and collected by recruiters. In a technical world, with high job prospects and little competition, the **FREE AGENT** is no longer a commodity on a shelf, but is now as hot as the smart phone in the palm of your hand.

Our predecessors may have had the guarantee of an income in their golden years, but you better believe that it came at a price. There is blood, sweat and tears invested in the thirty or 40 years years they gave to their employers to get that pension. What were they going to do? Quit? They couldn't for fear that they would lose everything. For some, life couldn't be better. For them, retiring with the certainty that they can keep up the lifestyle they have become accustomed to is worth any price. For others, it can be treacherous. It can be a thirty-year sentence with no early release for good behavior.

Keeping their head down and

mouth shut, playing by the rules

and keeping their eye on that

day, that day in the far off future

when they can say, "I'm done."

Not **FREE AGENTS**. We are

portable. What we may fail to

do is recognize how much we

have in common with the Free

Agents of professional sports:

- You have **TALENT**

- You produce measurable RESULTS

- You have great POTENTIAL

Is work your sport? Sport is defined as "a source of diversion[xiii]" Do you come prepared to play?

We tend to box ourselves into the daily rut of being a modern day white collar worker. We load up on caffeine, luxury cars and gadgets with little reflection on the game we play. To fully understand the industry you work in, the economy, the development of your own credibility and street worth is elusive to so many of us. We are going to tap into your inner **FREE AGENT**. We will learn from the Pros. Of course, there are always pre-requisites. You have to have the stomach to play the game. Not just anyone waltzes through the door of the Pittsburgh Steelers proclaiming they are here to play. It takes a

special breed, a competitive

spirit. It takes toughness, willing

to do and earn your stripes

because you know it's worth it.

Most of all, you have to enjoy it.

If you're the safe cubical dweller

that rarely emerges to top off

your Christmas mug in July, this

book is most likely not for you.

You keep doing what you're

doing and be happy. Safety and

security is your gin and tonic.

For those of you who enjoy

being daring, bold and brazen or

would like to become so, follow

me. Let's become **FREE**

AGENTs together.

Thoughts

- What talents to you bring to a team?
- How do you view yourself as the next up-and-coming Free Agent in your profession?
- Learn from others; even the Free Agents in professional sports need humility and they see every opportunity to join

a Winning Team as an

honor.

My Thoughts:

THE ROOKIE

Each year, sport fans crowd around to see the NFL Draft. We anxiously await the round-after-round announcements of players going to teams. Teams with poor records get their chance at high-talent players. Athletes get their chance to join the teams of their dreams. To see that athlete get their name called and join the suits on the stage to claim his jersey and hat is what is most memorable to me. He is now **PAID TO PLAY** and all the excitement, pride and anticipation of the next chapter in his pro life have just begun. Sound familiar? It should.

As undergraduates in the engineering colleges throughout our country, we are working, training and earning our credentials for that big graduation day. Our GPA is our Points per Game. Our co-op and internship experiences are our scouting season to show our raw potential on the field. You can bet as the resumes flow from every technical program in the country that you are being ranked and filed amongst the competition. The corporate giants that seek only the best have high standards. They will not consider you unless you meet their GPA requirements, period. They are highly selective, many looking for the right "fit" of capabilities and raw talent for long-term career potential. Our selection may be somewhat different but what remains the same is the competition for the entry-level slots in engineering. We compete for the best jobs with the best companies to gain that first job in engineering. Without that first job, many engineers fall by the sidelines and never truly get the opportunity to be PAID TO PLAY.

Even the most seasoned professionals can become the

Rookie again. In today's world of transitioning into new companies, roles or even career changers; the most experienced of professionals can find him or herself as a Rookie.

Now, forget and dismiss all the urban myths and legends of being at the bottom of the corporate ladder and needing thirty years to get respected in your profession. That is the old way of thinking and it simply does not exist anymore. It cannot. Not in our economy.

Companies need you to bring

everything you have to the table

from Day One. They cannot

afford to waste your talent by

forcing you to make copies and

get coffee for five years. If you

find yourself in that situation,

manage your boss. Share with

him or her why you joined the

company and what talents you

bring to the table. Keep it

respectful, but ask for more

responsibility. Just like LeBron,

your first job is where you start

building your reputation. Before

your first job, you are unknown.

You are unproven in the

professional world. This first

job is your opportunity to build

your stats of accomplishments.

Now, all that being said, you are

no longer the student who can

zone out during a lecture and

you are no longer under the

supportive hand of your mother.

As your employer, your

company will not be into hand-holding or coddling. They need and expect adult professional behavior. This is go-time with employers ready to leverage your skills and abilities. Don't mistake that interest in you for their willingness to take responsibility for your maturity. That is on you.

Tim Tebow, love him or hate him, brought leadership and maturity to the Denver Broncos from Day One. Despite being a twenty-something millennial, he is the leader of that team on and off the field.

This Rookie season of your technical career can be a very powerful way to set the stage for many years to come. Use this time wisely to learn all you can in the business you are in.

- Systems that run the business
- Management systems that support the business

- Sourcing, merchandising and marketing of products
- Industry strengths, weaknesses, opportunities and threats
- Competition and what they are investing in

Learn these aspects early in your career. Later, you will depend on this experience to determine how to approach the next opportunity. Without the development of your subject matter expertise, you will lack business acumen.

Developing your business

acumen is expected as a

Rookie. Failing to develop

your acumen for business

will hold you back from

becoming a Free Agent.

Communication skills are

extremely important here.

Beware of talking like you

have just left the hive of your

college campus. The "like,"

"um" and "sucks" need to be

practiced out of your

vocabulary. You need to be able to clearly communicate with a mature and confident voice. Challenge yourself to remove emotional comments and develop an active vocabulary. The professional world is no place for "mights", "maybe" or "hope" then they expect to get things done. Our words need to evoke action. Using the phrase, "we will, if..." can instill confidence to get things done, under the right conditions. Lay out the conditions to get things done and ask for help for meeting those conditions.

This is also the time to work on your confidence in play. One of my first managers would give me the coach pre-talk before a meeting. He would rally me to come prepared, think in advance of what I was going to say, what questions I had and challenge, challenge,

challenge the team to get things done and drive for results. It was unacceptable to attend a meeting just to attend a meeting. Don't show up to be a prisoner in the room, adding no value to the conversation, yet still sitting there, silent, throughout the entire meeting. If your presence is required, but you don't have the expertise to contribute, then volunteer to support the meeting. Be the scribe of the notes and publish them within 24 hours after the meeting. You will win hearts and minds for being the support person and for actively listening to the team. Don't be a tourist. Don't show up for face time, to look as though you are part of the solution for personal gain. You're either in, or you are out. Come prepared to play.

Come prepared to contribute.

This is also the time to build your commanding skills. As you build your expertise in systems, processes, procedures, and the business you will begin to see the opportunities and threats to success.

Making connections with other professionals is critical at this time. You may have a sharp and talented skill set that you immediately bring to the table, but you still need to develop partnerships and allies in the business. Learn from others and support the success of your boss, co-workers and teams. Be the ultimate support player by digging into the challenge, rolling up your sleeves, getting your hands dirty to earn that "Most Valuable Player" title. This effort will not go un-noticed. You will gain credibility, respect and fans. Be the workhorse for your team. Workhorses get it all done out of pure grit and glory.

Pete Rose was the ultimate **ROOKIE**. Pete as a young baseball player was full of the bravado and raw talent that baseball teams savored. Pete was once described in his early years as the "hardest worker in camp[xiv]." The hardest workers come in each day and contribute their 120%, not because they have to, but because they love what they do and enjoy doing what they do.

They are the architects of results.

They are making the big plays

happen.

He was ultimately known as the

"hardest worker in camp", for his

relentless work ethic and drive

to practice. It paid off. Pete in

his Rookie season became

Rookie of the Year and set his

feet firmly on the path of Most

Valuable Player and becoming

the highest paid baseball player

in 1979.

Very similar to the old baseball cards, we now have social media. These tools are very similar. The baseball cards had an image of the player striking the pose so they could be immediately recognized for who they are. The baseball cards had their name, background teams and stats for fans to collect and study their favorite players. The baseball cards served as a marketing tool to promote the popularity of

players with fans and drive
interest and a following.

Today, we have social media.
Sites like LinkedIn provide that
same snapshot of you as a
professional. You have your
image and description of your
track record. There is no
shortage of social media choices,
but beware. Social media is
immediately accessible, is
permanently displayed for all to
see, and can be a powerful tool
to market yourself or ruin your

credibility and career. Keep your social media for professional endeavors separate from your personal life. Facebook is one of the most popular and widely-used personal social media programs in the world. Keep it personal, make sure your settings are for "friends only" viewing and not "everyone." For professional social media, LinkedIn is the top choice. LinkedIn is your professional calling card of who you are, what you do, and your professional interests. Build your profile by getting a professional picture taken of yourself. Consider the payment of a few bucks to get a high quality picture as an investment. This will come in handy for any speaking engagements or award nominations that need your bio and picture. Manage your connections with people you trust. I only accept people into my connections that I have done business with, trust, and would recommend for a position. Your connections are a view of your online peer group or contemporaries --the quality of professionals you are associated with. Lastly, get and give recommendations. People you worked closely with can provide a succinct statement of your talent and how you demonstrated success working together. These are your online references that provide a view of

what you are capable of
providing. This builds your
potential equity.

Remember, the **ROOKIE** season
will not last forever. It is a rite of
passage for technical
professionals. Earn the degree,
get the first job, earn results,
and build your professional
network. This will position you
to become the next **FREE**
AGENT.

Thoughts

- How can I position myself to get my first job out of college?

- What can I learn in my first job?

- What can I do to take the initiative and provide for my team?

- How do I build my professional network? (Co-workers, Bosses, Customers, Clients)

- *Have I used social media wisely to provide a marketable and accurate image of me to the world?*

My Thoughts:

FREE AGENTS

For anyone who has played sports or even for us spectators, it's all about the stats. Besides, it is really a sport if there is no score? How do the players know how they did without Assists, Rebounds, or Three-Pointers? We relish stats. We savor the stats. The fact is, we get stats. We understand what they mean. We chart stats. We talk about the stats on Monday at the coffee pot. Many of us have played the national

pastime of Fantasy Football --

an estimated 32 million people

ages 12 and up in the U.S. and

Canada played this fantasy

sport in 2010[xvi].

Yet, time and time again, we fail

to use statistics to demonstrate

results in our own careers.

How do you win at your

profession?

How do you measure success?

Is your resume one of the hundreds that has passed by my desk that is barren of data or proof of excellence or impact?

Do you know how to win at your profession? Do you know if your business has been successful or a dismal failure?

Do you know the key performance indicators (KPIs) of your industry or business? Apparently even a 12-year-old knows the KPIs of football. You should know the basic statistics

of where you work.

FREE AGENTS know their

business. They build the

business acumen throughout

their careers. They gain an

understanding of the business

from a global perspective. They

learn how to measure success

in financial and operational

terms using the key

performance indicators (KPI) of

their company . **FREE AGENTS**

pepper their thinking,

conversation, actions, focus, energy, and resolve with stats that come from influencing the outcome of KPIs.

Have you made a percent improvement?

Have you saved millions of dollars?

Did you reap millions of dollars in sales?

Did you re-invent the industry or business process time by days, weeks, months, or years?

Learn how to **MEASURE**

ANYTHING.

How long did it take you to read
this book? (time) How many
words were in the book? (count)
What was the quality of the
content? (poor to excellent)

Anything we do can be
measured. If it can be
measured, it can be improved,
influenced, maximized, or
eliminated altogether.

Now, let's talk about the roles
that **FREE AGENTS** play.

Stats resonate for you and the
role you play. Stats quickly tell
the story that you're a **FREE
AGENT**. If it wasn't for your
involvement, participation,
thought leadership, or good old-
fashioned elbow grease, the
numbers would have been
different. Are you a **GAME
CHANGER**? Did you assemble,
participate and play on a
winning team? Did you lead the

charge of a team that took the

industry or company by storm,

providing the stats that have

never been achieved before?

Did you go for the big play, the

Hail Mary for your business or

mission, choosing to take risks

and bring about the

breakthrough that everyone

needed? This is the **FREE**

AGENT equity that you need on

your pedigree. Some of the best

FREE AGENTs in the white

collar world are the

"TURNAROUND SPECIALISTS."

These specialists are heavily sought-after professionals who take on the sick patient – ailing business deep in the red. They are swift and strategic, bold and brazen; they are **FREE AGENTS** who know that action is always better than being a victim. They act with expertise, experience, and courage that yield the results – the Michael Jordan of the business world. "Go big or stay home" is their mantra.

These are the **FREE AGENTS** of the elite business forces.

FREE AGENTS come in all aspects of the white collar world. A **FREE AGENT** can be the boots-on-the-ground specialist that takes charge, assumes responsibility, and acts to pull off the latest initiative, improvement, or design. Without him or her, simply put, things would not get done. In past years, these roles were looked over due to their "individual contributor" level of responsibility. Well, the technical time is here and brings with it a new breed of professional. Being the individual contributor today has a whole new meaning. We work in flat organizations with very few at the helm with managerial responsibilities. Today we see more individual contributors on special assignment or working across the organization. You might know them as:

BLACK BELTS

Project Managers

Specialists

These are the new internal consultants of organizations driving results on a large scale. Many of these **Free Agents** contribute tens of millions of dollars in value each year. They know their value, they know their peer group who share their abilities, and they leverage the opportunities that come their way.

Now, some **FREE AGENTS** may feel the bench from time to time. All of us take a turn being on the bench and supporting others. We may feel as if we are second- or third-string to someone else in the company. Being a backup can be a great strategic advantage to you.

Learn all you can; you must never stop learning.

Be supportive -- help and support the team's mission.

Use this time to hone and develop new skills.

One of the best stories of rising to the occasion and seizing the moment is that of pro football player Tom Brady. Despite playing football with the University of Michigan and leading them to an Orange Bowl win, Tom was selected as a second-string quarterback for the New England Patriots. After the starting quarterback Drew Bledsoe was hurt during a game,

Tom got his chance to step up and take the lead. Tom went on to lead the team to win the Superbowl and received the Most Valuable Player Award[xvii]. Tom took advantage of his opportunity to be the backup. He would not have had that success if he spent his time on the bench feeling sorry for himself or resenting the starting quarterback. Instead, the played the role he was in and stepped in when he was needed fully prepared and ready to play.

Now that we are **FREE AGENTS**, we have the advantage by showing what we do, how we do it, and proving it with tangible, measurable results. We go back to our baseball cards – LinkedIn, for example. Do not give away to your company's competitors what you are specifically doing! Rather, show the role, show the sum of the results.

"Game Changer capable of providing $20M in savings opportunities by improving service within a 6-month period."

You will begin to see a pattern of performance that spells out what you can truly bring to the table in your role.

Do you savor to get involved in projects that seem to languish in failure only to bring them about to closure with valued results? You are a Game Changer

Do you relish the opportunity to take a failing building or business on the verge of collapse and bring them back to a state of solvency? You are a Turnaround Specialist

Do you jump in, regardless of the situation, roll your sleeves up, quickly assess the situation and take on the role most needed to move forward?

You're a Team Player

Look for your patterns and

identify your role that makes you

unique and sets the fire in your

belly to get involved.

In your LinkedIn profile, use the

role that you have developed

and practiced within over time

as your calling card.

Don't just say "Automotive

Engineer," which tells the world

you can only play in the

automotive space (a

dramatically shrinking industry

compared to years past) and only as an engineer.

Instead, call yourself an "Engineering Professional," which opens your marketability to any industry. Engineering Professional can be used in any space; it offers flexibility and shows that you view yourself as the consummate professional in your career.

Find unique ways to pitch yourself that fits your strengths

and the roles you have most enjoyed and played at your highest level, versus simply a job title. Job titles can fence you in on your field of play.

By providing a professional view of yourself as a **FREE AGENT**, with tangible results to a wide audience , the unique and challenging opportunities will come to you. Be ready to play at your highest level.

Thoughts

- *Get data-driven from your experiences.*

- *Look for patterns and styles that you bring to the team.*

- *Choose your "keyboards" or "genres." Don't languish in vagueness; know what you do and what you want in broad enough terms to yield the most opportunities.*

- *Pull it together in one commanding statement about you.*

Your Thoughts:

CAREER WINS

Not only do we love our sports in America, but we love our coaches. We learn from an early age that the coach comes first. Some of America's most beloved coaches are remembered for the way the lived, the way they dressed, and -- of course -- their Career Wins.

We immediately think of Coach K (Krzyzewski) of the Duke Bluedevils and his 903 career wins (and counting!). Hoosiers still remain ever-loyal to The General, Bobby Knight, and his 902 career wins.

Just thinking of your efforts as Career Winnings tells the story of your Life's Mission. The truth is, every one of the coaches we hold to the highest honor for Career Wins have lost. The difference is, they are known and marketed for the Career Wins. Not their last play. We can learn from this. Take any resume of the white collar

workforce and what you will see

first is your last play.

Your last job.

Your last project or product.

How many recruiters,

headhunters, or others stop right

there and make a judgment call

of what you are all about.

Passing you over for the next

resume with the last play that

leaves a brighter impression?

What about your Career Wins?

What is your total years of experience?

What were significant milestones in your career?

What is the sum of your stats?

What is your calling card of the role you play at the highest level?

What do others say about you? Do you have recommendations from others?

Again, back in the Pension World, the tenure was enough

for street credibility and promotions. Not so with **FREE AGENTS**. Companies want results. Your results will lift your Free Agency. Now, do you know your **CAREER WINS**? Take a fresh look at your resume. For each role you have held and listed on your resume, you should have three key experiences loaded with stats. There is no way you can know your Career Wins if you have not been keeping score!

Tally your stats. Total dollars saved over your career. Total sales dollars over your career. Do you see a trend in your percent impact to the business or industry? Now you're starting to see something bigger. The accumulation of your career in stats. Powerful, isn't it? You probably didn't realize how much you have done in your career. You may see an emerging trend. Are you a

Game Changer? Are you a

Turnaround Specialist?

Now you know who you are and

what you have done in your

career. Now write down a

succinct statement that pulls that

together. Having a **CAREER**

WINNING STATEMENT at the

beginning of your resume will

set you apart immediately.

Some examples of Career

Winning Statements:

Proven technical professional with household names delivering over $ 100M in career operational savings

Leader of technical support teams spanning the globe to provide world class customer service

Turnaround Specialist bringing challenged organizations to rapid operational success in nine months or less

Six Sigma Champion to deploy

business strategies to reduce

cost of goods by 20% in less

than a year

These examples of Career

Winning Statements provide:

The role you play "Game

Changer"

The scale of your involvement,

"household names"

How results in this role are

summarized, "20% cost of

goods"

The Career Winning Statement is a succinct statement of you, your calling card and marketing ploy to the world that views you as a contemporary in your field.

You are putting your best foot forward as a **FREE AGENT**. It tells the story of what you have done, your history, your legacy in your field. Rather than being seen and passed over based on your last play, you are now projecting the image of what you have accomplished over time.

You are now taking charge of your career as a **FREE AGENT**. Ready to hear your name called to the Hall of Fame for your profession; the next Fellow, Distinguished Alumni, the consummation of your career coming to fruition for you to play at the highest level.

Technical Professionals with Career Wins are found in every aspect of the business world we live in. Any product on the shelf or service you enjoy has the fingerprints of technical professions on it. This is our time, spanning the globe of infrastructure renewal, service sectors, and commerce at the digital level. There are some arenas we have yet to make our biggest plays.

Education continues to be one of our greatest challenges in the United States, with budgets strapped for cash and escalating labor costs. Sound familiar? How is this any different than the businesses we support? It's not.

It's funding versus sales. It's still

a budget.

What is the educational sector

waiting for? The solution is

finding more money, not re-

engineering the problems. Here

we are, on the bench. We are

waiting for you to call our names.

What about our government? It

seems that each election

season we seek candidates with

experience from the corporate

world, hoping to bring that same

business savvy to Washington. Isn't our government the ultimate corporation of departments, budgets, and programs? How is that any different from corporations? It should not matter what wing you live in -- right wing, left wing, whatever. Don't we all want a nimble government that gets things done? Again, here we are, the technical professionals with Career Wins sitting on the bench, just waiting for that call.

Thoughts:

- *Determine your Career Winnings.*

- *Write your succinct Career Winning Statement.*

- *Play at the highest level and enjoy the peak season of your professional life.*

Your Thoughts:

Full Potential

It was several years ago when I was considering taking the plunge to go to engineering school. Of course I had a lot of encouragement and support from friends, family, and colleagues. I actually faced a lot of adversity. Most advice I received was to take on something easier. The advice being that engineering is perceived as too "hard". One of my engineering friends did share with me that all engineers shared one thing in common – potential. That engineers hold potential to work as the engineers, but also the ability to do so much more. Engineers have great potential to grow and run businesses. This potential keep me going when the going got tough. Believe me, it was tough most of the time. It's no secret that engineering has been rated as one of the top professions for generations.

The mechanical engineer was first noted as the top-paying professional as early as the 1900's. For decades, all facets of engineering have been listed as low stress and high-paying professionals. It's this earning potential that brings many to the doorsteps of the universities across America. For the **FREE AGENT**, it means a whole lot more. The **FREE AGENT** not only takes advantage of that first foot in the door, but will use that first experience to earn street credibility. No different from the draft picks in the NFL , engineers are hired out of college based on their collegiate results. GPA is king. The higher the GPA, the better the opportunities can be with some of the most prestigious teams, by which I mean companies in America. Do you want to work for Microsoft, Google, or General Electric? Well, you had better have done your best as an undergrad to make the cut.

They only hire the top graduates

across the country and abroad.

This white collar version of the

lottery pick happens every year

without fans and fame. The

FREE AGENT takes their new

venture as the opportunity to set

the table for the future. They do

whatever they need to do for

those first years to get tangible

experience. They learn the

business, the systems, and the

politics of getting things done.

Many start off in management or leadership development programs with their first employer. This provides rotational experiences as a fast track to learning the business. Then the results come. They begin learn how their company keeps score. This is a turning point. Many engineers never learn this. Pity them, for they are the ones who will struggle to be employed in the new economy. Other learn this late in their careers. It's good for them to see what it takes to have a career in a demanding economy. The **FREE AGENT** knows this innately. They take the jobs that nobody else wants. They will take the leadership role in a remote town. They see the opportunity to take turnaround opportunities, seize the chance to put points on the board early and fast. They keep track of their stats. They keep a fresh track record of their success. They keep an elevator speech about themselves in their mind. At any time, in any place, they could meet the connection that could lead to the next big opportunity. They can succinctly tell you their **CAREER WINNING STATEMENT** as a **FREE AGENT**. They know themselves, what they can do, love to do, and need to do, and they keep moving in that direction. Forget what they don't like to do or have no interest in.

No wasting their time.

So why change teams? Why did LeBron James leave the Cleveland Cavaliers to play for the Miami Heat? To be the best. To win a championship.

Money ... well, I'm sure money had something to do with it. But the bottom line is, the **FREE AGENT** ticks on the same elixir as the LeBrons of the world.

They want to work for the best.

They want to make a difference

to a company that is memorable, acknowledged, and envied by others. They want to propel their company up the Fortune 500 rankings, to be listed among the Most Admired and Best Places to Work. It's about being the best among the best. It's the same competitive spirit that is played everyday in professional sports. Only our jerseys are blue button-down oxfords.

Businesses know it too. They seek the best. Why? The **POTENTIAL** to do more.

Companies everyday are seeking talent for different reasons. Some are downsizing, growing or expanding into new markets. They seek the **FREE AGENT** to get them there. Not every company is in this competitive arena. For some companies, good is good enough. Not every team in the NBA gets the talent and attention that the Lakers receive.

Just like business, the

opportune time and place to

assemble the best team you can

is cyclical. The **FREE AGENT** is

poised and ready for the next

career opportunity.

The next opportunity lies around

the corner for all of us. The

potential to do more is being

able to repeat results in different

settings, situations, opportunities,

and challenges. It can be the

expertise or specialty of a highly

developed skill. Controls and maintenance engineering professionals are great examples of a highly specialized skill set that is in great demand with very lucrative opportunities.

FREE AGENTS that offer a diversified background with a proven track record of success are appealing due to their flexibility in being an all-around player. You can be placed anywhere within the organization and counted on to drive results. It is this potential to keep winning, scoring, and playing at the highest level that draws corporations to the **FREE AGENT**. Companies are facing global competition, rising cost of goods, and internal transformations. They need high-potential players to bring expertise into the team and contribute from Day One. Sometimes there is simply no time for development. Corporations need strength --

independent and proficient performers that can take the role and execute without needing hand-holding, guidance, or continuous assurance. This is the opportunity for high potential individuals to succeed in the game we play in our careers and advance their ability to be PAID TO PLAY.

Thoughts

- *Have you ever been on a winning team? What made the difference between winning and losing?*

- *Why would you choose to change teams? What is your motivation?*

- *What is your potential?*

My Thoughts:

Passing It On

Some of the most amazing and inspirational stories come from sports. Who could ever forget the movie *Remember the Titans*, when the coach made the difference to a town, community, and team. Or Sandra Bullock as she played the mother who saw great potential in a boy in *The Blind Side*. Throughout sports we see the stories unfolding in front us on screen, television, and print -- countless stories of courage and devotion.

These stories are inspiration to

help others achieve greatness

that they don't see in

themselves. The working world

should be no different. For the

past twenty years, there have

been countless management

books and classes teaching the

value of teamwork. Yet, it is still

a dog-eat-dog world out there.

We participate on teams, but

don't see ourselves as that

coach that makes the difference.

That would require heart. That
would require personally
investing in what we do with
everything we are. . That's hard
to do in a sell-out CEO world of
cut-and-run and pink slips. But
that is what we have to do.

We have a white collar world
that is quickly evolving. The first
generation of Americans to
grow up with technology in their
hands has entered the
workforce. The Millennial
Generation has come to town,

briefcase in hand, and working next to you. For some, it's an exciting time of anticipating offers. Opportunities abound based on their track record of success throughout college and life. For others, it's a humbling experience of absence. No jobs, no prospects in their chosen field. College debt waits for no one. They must find their niche in life quick. Many experienced in the workforce are making the hiring decisions.

What are you looking for?

Better yet, what are you **not** looking for?

Of course, you must be professional, play by the rules and regulations, but what would a coach do? Give feedback. Coaches give the gift of feedback. Interviewing is time-consuming, but for those vital few candidates, you can give them the glimmer of hope for a position. If you choose not to hire him or her, at a minimum

give the gift of feedback. Tell

him or her what she or he needs

to hear. That is what any good

coach would do.

Was their image not

professional?

Was it a lack of communication

ability?

Did they fail to provide any

meaningful contributions to their

story?

For the fortunate few who make the team, consider yourself the Team Captain. Take the **ROOKIE** under your wing. Make sure they know the rules of the game of work. You have nothing to lose but everything to gain. By being a mentor to a new hire, that person will never forget what you have done for them. A career can span a good thirty to forty years of your lifetime -- you will never know who you will be working with or for in the future. This Millennial could be your boss one day. Treat them fairly, show them the ropes, and help them to be respected as a contributor to the team. Do not let thee valuable skill set that impressed you in the interview go unnoticed or become idle. Nothing is worse than locker room behavior on the job. Don't deny it, you have seen it yourself. Jackasses who think they know everything walking around treating the

ROOKIES like little kids,

reminding them of their youth,

holding them back or setting

them up for failure. This

behavior happens in the

workplace for the same reason it

happens in the locker room: fear.

Fear of losing your position on

the team. Fear that the ROOKIE

might make them look bad or,

worse yet, outperform them!

Learn that surrounding yourself

with strong performers will boost

your Free Agency.

Support **FREE AGENTS** by

leveraging the awards and

honors of your field. Every

professional player in this book

has won many of the respected

awards of their fields.

ROOKIE OF THE YEAR

GOLDEN GLOVE

MOST VALUABLE PLAYER

These awards recognize

performance in the fields of

baseball, basketball and other

sports. Professional societies

exist for technical professionals from Professional Engineers (PEs), Federal Engineers, and within every field imaginable for engineers. These societies provide opportunities to awards and honors to recognize, celebrate, and provide a great distinction amongst your contemporaries of excellence, service, and commitment to playing at a higher level. The awards in sports are celebrated and expected. For professionals, an un-tapped opportunity to celebrate and recognize our contributions. Leveraging these celebrations of success provides visibility to technical professionals to the next generation. How many young women and men would actually get excited about a career in engineering if they read about the Most Valuable Player in technology?

Getting into the game, being prepared to play, summarizing

your wins and celebrating the

season. This is what has made

our sports great. Now it's our

turn to get out there and play!

Thoughts:

- *Feedback is a gift, be selective and give it in a timely manner and in private.*

- *Be the Team Captain: who can you support, teach, and influence?*

- *Who do you admire in your profession? What award or honor can you nominate him or her for?*

Your Thoughts:

About the Author

Karla Tankersley is a technical professional with over twenty years of experience working for household names such as General Motors, Home Depot and Kroger. She is alumnae of the University of Cincinnati, College of Engineering. Karla is an active volunteer and leader for the Society of Women Engineers.

BIBLIOGRAPHY

LeBron James, King on and off the
Court, Ken Rapporport

Pete Rose, Baseball's All-Time
Greatest Hitters, David Jordan

Tom Brady, An Unauthorized
Biography, Belmont & Belcourt
Biographies

REFERENCES

[i] "Going for 50", LeBron James, King on and Off the Court, Ken Rappoport, Enslow Publishers, 2006, pg. 95

[iii] "Rookie Season", LeBron James, King on and Off the Court, Ken Rappoport, Enslow Publishers, 2006, pg. 58

[v] LeBron James stats, ESPN.com

[ix] Bureau of Labor Statistics, US Department of Labor, News Release, USDL-12-0012

[xi] Occupational Outlook Handbook, 2010-11 Edition, Bureau of Labor Statistics

[xii] Occupational Outlook Handbook, 2010-11 Edition, Bureau of Labor Statistics, Projections Data

[xiii] Webster Dictionary

[xiv] Pete Rose, Baseball's All-Time Greatest Hitter, David Jordan, Pg 20

[xvi] Wikipedia, Fantasy Sport, Size of Hobby

[xvii] Biography.com, Tom Brady

www.ingramcontent.com/pod-product-compliance
Lightning Source LLC
Chambersburg PA
CBHW072026190526
45166CB00015B/519